WEREWOLVES

CYNTHIA A. ROBY

Cavendish
Square

New York

CREATURES OF FANTASY
WEREWOLVES

BY

CYNTHIA A. ROBY

CAVENDISH SQUARE PUBLISHING · NEW YORK

Published in 2016 by Cavendish Square Publishing, LLC
243 5th Avenue, Suite 136, New York, NY 10016

Copyright © 2016 by Cavendish Square Publishing, LLC

First Edition

Website: cavendishsq.com

This publication represents the opinions and views of the author based on his or her personal experience, knowledge, and research. The information in this book serves as a general guide only. The author and publisher have used their best efforts in preparing this book and disclaim liability rising directly or indirectly from the use and application of this book.

CPSIA Compliance Information: Batch #WS15CSQ

All websites were available and accurate when this book was sent to press.

Library of Congress Cataloging-in-Publication Data

Roby, Cynthia A., author.
Werewolves / Cynthia A. Roby.
pages cm. — (Creatures of fantasy)
Includes bibliographical references and index.
ISBN 978-1-50260-510-8 (hardcover) ISBN 978-1-50260-511-5 (ebook)
1. Werewolves—Juvenile literature. 2. Werewolves—Folklore—Juvenile literature. I. Title.

GR830.W4R63 2015
398.24'54—dc23

2015006922

Editorial Director: David McNamara
Editor: Kristen Susienka
Copy Editor: Rebecca Rohan
Art Director: Jeffrey Talbot
Designer: Joseph Macri
Senior Production Manager: Jennifer Ryder-Talbot
Production Editor: Renni Johnson
Photo Research: J8 Media

Printed in the United States of America

CONTENTS

INTRODUCTION

Wolves are the ancestors of domestic dogs. They were first tamed by ancient hunter-gatherers.

Since the first humans walked Earth, myths and legends have engaged minds and inspired imaginations. Ancient civilizations used stories to explain phenomena in the world around them: the weather, tides, and natural disasters. As different cultures evolved, so too did their stories. From their traditions and observations emerged creatures with powerful abilities, mythical intrigue, and their own origins. Sometimes, different cultures encouraged various manifestations of the same creature. At other times, these creatures and cultures morphed into entirely new beings with greater powers than their predecessors.

Today, societies still celebrate the folklore of their ancestors—in films such as *The Hobbit, Maleficent,* and *X-Men*; and in book series such as Harry Potter and The Lightning Thief. Some even believe these creatures truly existed, and continue to walk the earth as living creatures. Others resign these beings to myth.

In the Creatures of Fantasy series, we celebrate captivating stories of the past from all around the world. Each book focuses on creatures both familiar and unknown: the **cunning** leprechaun, the valiant Pegasus, the towering giant, and the cursed werewolf. Their various incarnations throughout history are brought to life. All have their own origins, their own legends, and their own influences on the imagination today. Each story adds a new perspective to the human experience, and encourages people to revisit tales of the past in order to understand their presence in the modern age.

Delusions of becoming a wolf or other feared animal are universal.

1

THE MAN, THE WOLF

"Think wolf; be wolf."

KAT KRUGER, *THE NIGHT HAS CLAWS*

THE WOLF IS PERHAPS MAN'S OLDEST ENEMY. The relationship between the two reaches back into the dim and distant past. Our earliest ancestors both feared and admired the wolf, and often competed with the beast for food. Man feared the wolf's ferocity but admired its cunning. Man feared its **predatory** instinct but admired its stealth and swiftness. Man also feared its strength and tirelessness but admired its hunting prowess. The wolf was the ultimate enemy, yet man wished to imitate this predatory **canid**.

Many early hunters attempted to take on some of the wolf's characteristics. By adopting the wolf's techniques, they believed they could become better hunters and defenders against other

Opposite: Man and wolf have coexisted for centuries. Pictured is a cave painting of a prehistoric wolf.

predators. Man and wolf began to merge in the early mind. This was a part of an overall longing to be similar to the creature that successfully shared man's environment. But how could man take on the characteristics of such an animal? The answer seemed to be "by supernatural means."

A Love-Hate Relationship

Wolves are a lot like men. They are powerful, aggressive, territorial, and predatory. They are smart, curious, cooperative, loyal, and adaptable. They contribute to and respect the **ecosystems** they inhabit. Yet despite these similarities, man has historically had a problem with wolves.

Perhaps it is the ancient dispute over territory and food. Perhaps it is a type of jealousy that breeds misunderstanding. Whatever the reasons, humans seem to have always been at war with wolves.

The Days of the Dog

Wolves and early dogs were outstanding hunters with great appetites. The wolf was domesticated, or tamed, at a time when modern humans were not tolerant of **carnivorous** competitors. In fact, after modern humans arrived in Europe around forty-three thousand years ago, they wiped out almost every large carnivore that existed. This included saber-toothed cats and giant hyenas. The **fossil record** does not reveal whether these large carnivores starved to death because modern humans took most of the meat from them. It is possible that humans killed them off on purpose. Either way, most of the Ice Age **bestiary** became extinct.

Within the illustration:

Waarhafftige Begebenheit!
Mit einem Verbannten Wolff; welcher im 1685sten Jahr im
Marggrafthum Onolzbach etliche Kinder Weggetragen und ge-
fressen, lezlich den 9 Octobris in einem brünen zu Neüses, boy Eschen-
bach gefangen, und ertödet: so dann, dieser figur nach, auffgehangen Worden,

Neüses

Eschenbach

Les Loups de Paris

Wolves began to invade Paris during the Hundred Years' War (1337–1453). Called *Les Loups de Paris*, meaning "The Wolves of Paris," the pack was so starved that it fed on the bodies of the recently buried in villages and fields. At night, scavenging wolves roamed the villages. They attacked, killed, and ate people. During the summer of 1423, several were captured within Paris. The situation became worse from 1436 to 1440.

In the Paris region, wolves came out of the forests to roam the countryside for months on end. In the summer of 1438, the beasts returned to Paris for a second time, attacking and eating several people. Charles VII, King of France, wrote in *Chronique*: "There were so many wolves in the areas around Paris that it was astonishing, some of them ate people."

By the end of 1438, bloodthirsty packs of wolves terrorized the paths alongside France's Seine River. They snatched dogs and devoured children. In 1439, more Parisians became victims of the wolves' violent behavior. There seemed to be no relief in sight. Panicked residents were under siege. They gave a nickname to the

Parisians trap and kill *Les Loups de Paris*.

pack's alpha male, or leader: Courtard, meaning Bobtail. He was named so because his tail was shorter than that of other wolves, which made him stand out. Eventually though, Parisians had enough of being fearful. The hunters would soon become the hunted.

A scheme was concocted to kill Courtard and his murderous pack. A large group of Parisians lured the wolves onto the isolated Ile de La Cité, a natural island within the city of Paris. The crowd, in the public square in front of Notre Dame Cathedral, then stoned and speared the entire pack to death. No doubt Courtard's distinctive tail was taken as a trophy.

Centuries of Persecutions

Over the last few centuries, almost every culture has hunted wolves to extinction. The first documented record of the wolf's persecution was in the sixth century BCE. It was then that Solon of Athens, a lawmaker, offered a bounty for every wolf killed. He paid five silver drachmas (the basic monetary unit of Greece, circa 1831–2001) to any hunter for killing any male wolf, and one drachma for every female. In 950 in England, King Athelstan made a ruling that Welsh king Hywel Dda receive three hundred wolf skins each year. Criminals were also ordered to provide a certain number of wolf tongues to Dda. If they refused or fell short of their quota, the criminals were put to death.

The Norman kings (reigning from 1066–1154 CE) employed servants as wolf hunters. William the Conqueror granted the lordship of Redesdale in Northumberland to Robert de Umfraville, who was to defend the land from enemies and wolves. King John of England (reined 1199–1216) gave ten shillings, or British coins, for the capture of two wolves. King Edward I of

Over centuries, many wolves have been hunted.

England (reigned 1272–1307) ordered the total extermination of all wolves in his kingdom.

James I, King of Scotland, passed a law in 1427 requiring three wolf hunts each year. These events were to take place between April 25 and August 1, as these dates coincided with cub-hunting season—the part of hunting season where young hounds were trained by killing wolf cubs.

The wolf became extinct in England during the reign of Henry VII (1485–1509). However, wolves survived in Scotland up until the eighteenth century. It is said that Mary, Queen of Scots, hunted wolves in the forest of Atholl in 1563. But none of the stories about the killing of the last wolf of Scotland can be confirmed.

Official records show that the last Scottish wolf was killed in 1680 by Sir Ewan Cameron of Lochiel, a Scottish highland chieftain. Yet folklore tells us that MacQueen of Pall à Chrocain, a legendary highland deer stalker, killed Scotland's last wolf in 1743. Wolves in North America were not safe from hunters either. By 1930, there were no wolves left in the forty-eight contiguous, or touching, states.

In animal form, werewolves seem like any other wolf.

A Tale of the She-Wolf

In the mountains of Auvergne—a historic province in south central France—a story dating back to 1588 was told of a royal female werewolf. In the story, a nobleman was gazing from the window of his chateau. Upon seeing a huntsman he knew, the nobleman beckoned him to the chateau. He wanted to know about details of his hunt. What the nobleman learned changed his life. The story is as follows.

While in the forest—but not very deep—a huntsman stumbled upon a wolf. The two struggled; the hunter **severed** one of the wolf's paws and placed it in his pouch as a trophy. Upon being beckoned to the nobleman's chateau, the huntsman exposed his gruesome prize. He opened his pouch to show evidence of the encounter with the wolf. When both men looked inside the pouch, what they discovered was not a paw at all—inside was a feminine hand bearing an elegant gold ring. The nobleman, recognizing the ring, sent the huntsman away and sought for his wife. When he went came upon her in the kitchen, he found her nursing a wounded arm. He removed the bandage only to find that her hand had been cut off.

Upon questioning her, she finally admitted to being the wolf with which the huntsman had fought. The wife's confession marked her for certain execution. In a matter of days, Isabelle of France, as she was known, was burned at the stake.

2

TALES OF THE WEREWOLF

"Whoever is bitten by a werewolf and lives becomes a werewolf himself."
MALEVA (PLAYED BY MARIA OUSPENSKAYA), *THE WOLF MAN* (1941)

THE ORIGIN OF THE WEREWOLF SUPERSTITION is unknown, yet its legend is ancient and widespread. It is an old and primitive tale told in regions throughout the world. The common thread in all of these stories is the transformation of a living human being into a wolf.

Stories of werewolves can be found as far back as history has been written. Tales of these **shape-shifter** myths can be heard all over the world, from China to Iceland and Brazil to Haiti. Some of the earliest tales of werewolves come from Romania and Greece. In many of these stories, being sentenced to life as a werewolf was a curse.

Opposite: This illustration from the 1941 story "The Werewolf Howls" shows a werewolf in a cemetery, one of their favorite places.

Myths of Transformations

In parts of the world where other animals dominated as predators, myths of shape-shifters are rampant. In Africa, for example, a person may be transformed into a lion, hyena, or leopard; in India, a tiger or serpent. Among Lapps and Finns (inhabitants of Finland) are stories of transformations into bears, reindeer, fish, or birds. Among many North Asiatic peoples, or Native Americans, people change into the bear. In South America, it is said that people change into a tiger or jaguar, a fish or a serpent. But the stories of the commonest animal, the wolf, have remained throughout history and have grown into tales of the werewolf.

Origin of Superstitions

The ultimate origins of the werewolf are indeed obscure and lost in ancient mythology. It is thought that the origin of the superstition was an old custom of primitive cultures. People would put on a wolf's or other animal's skin. Sometimes, masks were worn. These methods were used to lure animals into a trap. Some could be tempted by bait such as food; others were more easily drawn to their own kind. If a man dressed, for example, in a wolf's skin, he could get close enough to a wolf to attack it with his club, stone, or other weapon. Thus the animal disguise was used to secure food and clothing.

Some attribute the origin of **lycanthropy** to primitive **totemism** in which the totem is an animal revered by the members of a tribe. This particular animal is supposed to be hostile to their enemies. Others explain that the leader of "all departed souls" is the original werewolf.

The first use of the word "werewolf" occurs in English. It is written in the Ecclesiastical Ordinances of Cnut, a Danish king who ruled a great part of England between 1017 and 1035. It is believed to come from two Old English words: *wer*, meaning "man," and *wulf*, meaning "wolf." Some scholars argue that there are other possible root words: the Old English *weri* and *wulf*, meaning "wearer of wolf skin." *Vargulf* or *wargwulf* are ancient Scandinavian and English names for an outlaw wolf that receives pleasure in killing.

When the Moon Is Full

To precisely define the werewolf is not easy. The **lycan**, or werewolf, is a human—man, woman, or child—who morphs, or transforms, into a ferocious and bloodthirsty wolf-like beast, usually during a full moon. Changing into this creature can be voluntary or involuntary, depending on the culture. The shape-shifter then takes on the characteristics of a wolf: the foul appetite, the ferocity and cunning, brute strength, and swiftness. The werewolf is a combination of deadly sharp teeth and nails, and develops an abnormal amount of hair growth over the body. During the night, the beast lunges from graveyards, **moors**, forests, and alleyways to attack its victims.

This shape-shifting is, for the most part, temporary, yet it can sometimes be permanent. It can come into being by specific rites and

The full moon has long been associated with the transformation of humans to werewolves.

ceremonies; it is hereditary or acquired. One can experience the horrible pleasure of being born with a thirst for human blood. Other times, the transformation can be a punishment or source of revenge.

Lycaon and Jupiter

Publius Ovidius Naso, better known as Ovid, was a Roman poet remembered for his fifteen-book, twelve-thousand-line poem, "Metamorphoses." This work, written in Latin around 8 CE, is a collection of mythological and legendary stories. Many are taken from Greek sources.

From the creation of the universe to the death of Julius Caesar, the stories in "Metamorphoses" are told in order. Common themes in many of Ovid's stories are obedience and disobedience toward the gods. Mythical characters are used to illustrate these themes. They are either rewarded or punished for their actions by undergoing a final transformation into some type of animal, vegetable, or cosmic form.

Hoping it false I left Olympus's heights, and travelled the earth, a god in human form. It would take too long to tell what wickedness I found everywhere. Those rumours [sic] were even milder than the truth.

In "Metamorphoses," Ovid tells of the god Jupiter, who has heard rumors about awful and inconsiderate human behavior. Jupiter wants to witness this himself, so he comes to Earth disguised as a man. He is treated terribly everywhere he goes, so he decides to travel to the land of Arcadia, where he plans to reveal himself as a god. It is only then that the people begin to worship and respect him—all but the Arcadian king, Lycaon, who is known as a tyrant.

Lycaon does not believe Jupiter to be a true god, so he sets out to test him. His plan is to murder Jupiter in his sleep. This will certainly prove Jupiter's mortality. But first, Lycaon murders an emissary from a nearby tribe. Lycaon cuts the man's throat, takes some parts of the victim, and boils them. He roasts other parts over the fire. Lycaon serves this poisonous dish to Jupiter during a supper in honor of his presence. Yet Jupiter is a god and thereby sees through Lycaon's murderous attempt:

Jan Cossiers's *Júpiter y Licaón* (Jupiter and Lycaon)

> But no sooner had he placed these before me on the table than I, with my avenging bolt, o'er threw the house upon its master and on his guilty household. [Lycaon] himself flies in terror and, gaining the silent fields, howls aloud, attempting in vain to speak. His mouth of itself gathers foam, and with his accustomed greed for blood he turns against the sheep, delighting still in slaughter. His garments change to shaggy hair, his arms to legs. He turns into a wolf, and yet retains some traces of his former shape. There is the same grey hair, the same fierce face, the same gleaming eyes, the same picture of beastly savagery.

Jupiter is outraged upon discovering the tainted dish. **Cannibalism** is frowned upon in that part of the world and considered a punishable offense. Jupiter then flattens Lycaon's palace with a thunderbolt, drives Lycaon out into the wild, and turns him into a wolf—permanently. Because Lycaon obviously prefers human flesh, the wolf form, according to Jupiter, is a more suitable form of existence. From the name Lycaon came the word "lycanthrope," meaning "one who transforms into a wolf."

The Werewolf of Bedburg

Peter Stubbe (or Stuppe, Stumpp, or Stumpf) was a prosperous farmer who lived just outside Bedburg, a small city in Germany's Rhineland. Bedburg had been devastated during the Cologne War (1583–1588). It was during this time that townspeople began turning up dead.

Among the townspeople were rumors of a wolf-like creature roaming the countryside, killing both humans and animals. The beast was described as "greedy … strong and mighty, with eyes great and large, which in the night sparkled like unto brands of fire, a mouth great and wide, with most sharp and cruel teeth, a huge body and mighty paws."

Fed up with the killings, in 1589, a group of men accompanied by their hounds went into the forest to destroy the creature. They tracked the beast down and encircled it. But when they moved in for the kill, the wolf seemed to have disappeared. Stubbe was there instead. It is unknown whether the hunters witnessed Stubbe transform back from being a wolf, or if he was in the wrong place at the wrong time. Either way, under the threat of torture, he confessed to the murders of sixteen people. Before the townspeople put Stubbe to death on October 31, 1589, it was found that he owned a belt made of wolf's skin that turned him into a werewolf when he wore it—hence the name "the Werewolf of Bedburg."

Laignech Falead

As the civilizations of the world began to develop and grow, folklore grew and developed with them. Among the most widely spread of these tales was that of the werewolf. For example, up until the fourteenth century, there was a belief in Ireland that a tribe of werewolves roamed about the County Tipperary. This clan of wolf-men was known as the *Laignach Faelad*.

In many Irish tales, as well as the Irish text known as the *Cóir Anmann*, the Laignach Faelad were described as half man, half wolf. They were brutal soldiers dressed in wolf skins who showed no mercy to those who crossed their path. For a steep price, the inhuman beasts would fight a bloody battle for any Celtic king of Ireland. Their steep price, however, was neither money nor gold. They demanded the flesh of newborns, which they divided among themselves and devoured raw. Any king known to have hired the Laignach Faelad was thought to be ruthless and desperate.

The Laignach Faelad were followers of Crom Cruach, one of the oldest and most bloodthirsty of Irish deities. It is said that these ancient warriors were the most powerful during the reign of King Tigernmas, meaning "lord of death" in Old Irish. Tigernmas was also a follower of this god.

Later, in the sixteenth century, English historian William Camden dismissed the tale of the Laignach Faelad, saying that "the Wolf Men of Tipperary never lived." However, no one has ever proven the tale to be false.

3

TRANSFORMING FOLKTALES

*"The wolf is carnivore incarnate and he's as cunning as he is ferocious;
once he's had a taste of flesh then nothing else will do."*

ANGELA CARTER, "THE COMPANY OF WOLVES"

FOLKTALES CONCERNING PEOPLE WHO could transform themselves into wolves and speak with a human voice were especially popular in France. The most widely known of these tales is Charles Perrault's "Petit Chaperon Rouge" ("Little Red Riding Hood"), written in 1697. In the story, a wolf talks to Little Red Riding Hood and then dresses in her grandmother's clothing to fool her.

Perrault's stories in *Mother Goose* (1697) were written solely to entertain his children. They include "Petit Chaperon Rouge," "The Sleeping Beauty," "Puss-in-Boots," and "Bluebeard," and modern versions of half-forgotten folktales.

Opposite: In this 1883 painting by French artist Gustave Doré, a frightened Red Riding Hood realizes that the wolf has eaten her grandmother.

Little Red Riding Hood

In the original narrative of "Little Red Riding Hood," Red Riding Hood journeys through the forest to take her sick grandmother a basket of food. Dressed in a red cape, she meets a wolf who wants to talk to and, perhaps, eat her:

> The Wolf asked her where she was going. The poor child, who did not know that it was dangerous to stay and talk to a wolf, said to him, "I am going to see my grandmother and carry her a cake and a little pot of butter from my mother."

The cunning wolf now has the exact directions to Red Riding Hood's grandmother's house. He also knows that the grandmother is both ill and housebound. Red Riding Hood takes the longer path, picking wildflowers and chasing butterflies along the way. The wolf, however, has mischievous plans, and takes the shorter path. He arrives at the grandmother's house, and changes his voice.

Charles Perrault

The grandmother is tricked into believing that Red Riding Hood has arrived:

> He knocked at the door: tap, tap.
> "Who's there?"
> "Your grandchild, Little Red Riding Hood," replied the wolf, counterfeiting her voice; "who has brought you a cake and a little pot of butter sent you by Mother."
> The good grandmother, who was in bed, because she was somewhat ill, cried out, "Pull the bobbin, and the latch will go up."

In this illustration by Alfred L. Sewell, Little Red Riding Hood meets the Big Bad Wolf in the forest.

The wolf pulled the bobbin, and the door opened, and then he immediately fell upon the good woman and ate her up in a moment, for it been more than three days since he had eaten. He then shut the door and got into the grandmother's bed, expecting Little Red Riding Hood, who came some time afterwards and knocked at the door: tap, tap.

There he waits for Red Riding Hood to arrive—and when she does, the wolf pretends to be the bedridden grandmother:

"Who's there?"

Little Red Riding Hood, hearing the big voice of the wolf, was at first afraid; but believing her grandmother had a cold and was hoarse, answered, "It is your grandchild, Little Red Riding Hood, who has brought you a cake and a little pot of butter Mother sends you."

The wolf cried out to her, softening his voice as much as he could, "Pull the bobbin, and the latch will go up."

Little Red Riding Hood pulled the bobbin, and the door opened.

The wolf, seeing her come in, said to her, hiding himself under the bedclothes, "Put the cake and the little pot of butter upon the stool, and come get into bed with me."

Little Red Riding Hood took off her clothes and got into bed.

Red Riding Hood notices that her grandmother appears different. She comments on the size of her of arms, legs, ears, eyes, mouth, and teeth.

Sadly, there is no happy ending to this tale: "And, saying these words, this wicked wolf fell upon Little Red Riding Hood, and ate her all up."

The Werewolves of Poligny

Perrault adopted "Little Red Riding Hood" from the legend of the werewolves of Poligny, a sixteenth-century folktale. A traveler was passing through the town of Poligny, France, when a werewolf attacked him. The two fought, leaving the werewolf wounded. A trail of the shape-shifter's blood led the traveler to a cottage in the woods.

Inside the cottage were a man and wife. The wife was bandaging a wound on the man's arm. The traveler became suspicious and reported the incident to the authorities. A man named Michel Verdun was soon arrested. He confessed to being a shape-shifter as well as committing **heinous** crimes such as murder and cannibalism. He also gave up the names of two other shape-shifters, Pierre Bourgot and Philibert Montot. Both admitted to

eating human flesh. They also confessed that they had been given an ash-colored powder that, when rubbed into the skin of the left arm, allowed them to disappear if they encountered any animal in the wild.

Yet according to Johan Wier, a sixteenth-century defender of witches, the confessions were likely forced. He also pointed out that the accused answered the same questions in confused and varying ways. Nevertheless, all three men were brought to trial, executed, and burned. The trio became known as the werewolves of Poligny.

The tower in the old town in Poligny, France, where three shape-shifters were brought to trial and executed

Berserkers battled in an uncontrollable, trance-like fury, and were alleged to be able to perform seemingly impossible superhuman feats of strength.

BERSERKERS

The **Vikings** told tales of berserkers, ferocious warriors who devoured the flesh of their slain victims and smeared themselves in their victims' blood. It is from these people that the word "berserk," meaning "uncontrollable," originates. The word berserk itself comes from two root sources: "ber" from the animal itself, the bear, and "serker," meaning shirt. This meaning suggests that to make their appearance more ferocious and to terrify their enemies, some of these berserkers wore animal skins.

Extremely fearless and vicious in battle, berserkers were described as those who "went without their mail coats and were mad as hounds or wolves, bit their shields, and were as strong as bears or bulls. They slew men but neither fire nor iron had effect upon them." These slayings were called *berserkganger*, meaning "going berserk."

One thirteenth-century tale of a berserker is that of Thorolf Halt-Foot. According to legend, after his death, Halt-Foot rose from his tomb night after night. Accompanied by several of the undead, they ravaged much of the countryside of Western Iceland, attacking flocks of sheep and, from time to time, people. Thorolf Halt-Foot became such a menace that his son was forced to erect a wall around his grave in order to keep him locked inside.

It is believed that over time, the idea of fierce warrior cults draped in bear or wolf skins strengthened the links between man and beast. This added considerably to the idea that a man might transform himself into an animal.

4

MYTHOLOGY AND POWERS

"My transformations in those days were terrible. It is very painful to turn into a werewolf ... The villagers heard the noise and the screaming and thought they were hearing particularly violent spirits."

REMUS LUPIN, *HARRY POTTER AND THE PRISONER OF AZKABAN*

MANY MYTHS SURROUND WEREWOLVES regarding their powers. They have the ability to shape-shift and savagely attack victims using superhuman strength. They can communicate with and call forth the ancestral werewolf spirits. Werewolves possess superhuman agility. Even in human form they are quite acrobatic and run incredibly fast without difficulty or exhaustion. These and more tales of the lycan's powers make it one of the most feared and unpredictable beasts in mythology.

WOLVES AND WITCHES

Today, most people consider witches and werewolves separate kinds of supernatural beings. However, throughout the latter half

Opposite: Werewolves, such as *Teen Wolf*'s Tyler Posey, have many powers, including shape-shifting.

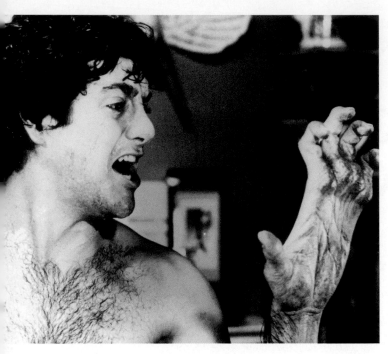

The process of shifting can be painful.

of the sixteenth and most of the seventeenth century, many people considered them one and the same. During this time, many people thought witches ran **amuck**. To the superstitious, they held many magical powers, one being the ability to transform themselves into other forms, usually those of animals.

During the twelfth century, Welsh-born Gerald de Barri became the first foreigner to write a book about Ireland. In it he wrote that it was within the power of all Irish women to change themselves into hares and stoats in order to drink milk from the udders of cows. (This belief was still held in many Irish rural areas at the beginning of the twentieth century.) Soon, animal transformations had become part of people's beliefs about witches.

According to legend, witches roamed the countryside dressed as animals. They did so to harm their neighbors without being recognized. They used potions and **unguents** to transform themselves into stoats, weasels, cats, ravens, and other creatures. Dressed as horses, witches trampled crops and broke down fences. Disguised as mice, they gnawed through grain sacks. The forms they took on and the havoc they wreaked were endless. It was not long before witches began to transform into wolves, as they recognized the beasts' power.

Painful Shifting

Any human who transforms into a wolf is also known as a lycan. All lycans must endure "shifting" to assume their wolf-like form. This process is usually described as very painful. Tissue and flesh are torn apart, bones are broken, and muscles are reshaped. Because of this, many horrifying screams and howls sound early in a werewolf's transformation. Legend says that the torture of shifting fuels the lycan's rage and increases its strength. This is when the beast begins to salivate at the prospect of devouring human flesh.

In the 1947 fictional story "Eena," author Manly Banister described a she-wolf's transformation:

> The sun came up over the shoulder of the mountain and tinged the lake with blood. And Eena changed. It was no sensation of pleasure to return to the wolf. Eena felt the agony of the change in every muscle and nerve. She screamed with the horrid crunching and grinding of bones in her head, lengthening into the lupine muzzle. Albino fur sprouted like a million thorny barbs from her tender skin.

As traditional stories go, returning to human state in the morning, however, is easier for the lycan because in most cases, it has passed out. The rising sun causes the werewolf to weaken, so it moves quickly and seeks cover in wooded areas, ditches, caves, or other abandoned areas. At that point, the lycan must sleep and typically does not wake for hours.

The shape-shifter wakes groggy and disoriented, usually undressed and in a location that is unknown. There is no pain from the shifting. In fact, the shape-shifter feels energized and full of

life following a night of mayhem. Sometimes a shifter experiences random flashbacks of the ravaging that took place during the full moon.

Strength, Speed, Resilience

All shape-shifters, upon their first change, are gifted with increased and enhanced physical strength. The average werewolf can lift a car over his or her head or even punch right through a cement wall.

Werewolves possess the natural ability to move at greater speeds than both humans and vampires—and they do so gracefully. Oftentimes they move at speeds that exceed 60 miles (96.6 kilometers) per hour. They are so fast that they appear only as a blur. A werewolf's strength and speed peak during a full moon.

Compared to humans, werewolves are resilient creatures. Beatings, gunshot wounds, and deep cuts don't stop them. Put simply, a lycan can take far more punishment than a human, all the while remaining upright and dangerous.

Super Senses and Regenerative Powers

The senses of werewolves are at a heightened state. They can clearly hear sounds at a great distance. They can smell fear, lust, and even the scent of a liar. It takes time and experience to identify all the scents, but they know when a scent is present. Lycans also have the ability to smell groups of predatory animals as well as other shifters or werewolves.

According to myth, lycans heal themselves, and they do so very quickly in most cases. They can self-heal wounds inflicted by silver and the teeth and claws of vampires or other lycans.

The Silver Bullet

According to the agents of the Spanish Inquisition, there is only one way to kill a werewolf: cut off its head. Then, to be certain that the beast is dead, the head and the body must be burned. But what about the silver bullet, which has been established as another effective way to kill a werewolf?

Scriptwriter Curt Siodmak, who wrote the 1941 version of *The Wolf Man*, took credit for adding new details to the werewolf mythology—one being that an object made of silver or a silver bullet were the only items that could kill a werewolf. In the centuries-old struggle with werewolves, only one record of a silver-bullet slaying exists. This was during the reign of terror caused by the Beast of Gévaudan, a mythical creature that was held responsible for at least one hundred human deaths and sixty animal deaths in 1760s France. According to Jean Chastel, the man given credit for slaying the beast, he had loaded his double-barreled musket with bullets made from a silver chalice, or goblet. The bullets, Chastel said, were fatal to evil creatures because the chalice had been blessed by a priest. The goblet having been made from silver was simply a coincidence.

According to the tradition of medieval chemical science, silver represents the moon, purity, and chastity. According to the Merriam-Webster dictionary, the term "silver bullet" is "something that acts as a magical weapon; one that instantly solves a long-standing problem." Hence the silver bullet is the perfect weapon against the ferocious werewolf.

Forced Confessions

Lycanthropy was considered a form of witchcraft because it involved **heresy**. People in fifteenth-century France feared that strange magical

Many innocent people in sixteenth-century France were burned at the stake.

things were happening to others and against them. The fear turned into hysteria and spread quickly. When a brutal and gruesome crime was committed, werewolves were immediately suspected.

By the sixteenth century, the secular (nonreligious) courts had adopted inquisition, or examination, procedures to protect society from witches and werewolves. In 1532, judicial torture became an acceptable means to determine whether vicious acts were committed by the use of witchcraft or lycanthropy.

Whether a person had cast a spell was not something that could be proven. Thus the only way to prove guilt was by confession. The best way to force an acknowledgment of guilt was to apply brutal and savage force. Inquisitors who heard confessions found it difficult to believe the inhuman and sadistic horrors of the crimes. They preferred to think of them as having been committed by a true monster: one that was half man and half wolf. As a result, many people who confessed to these horrible acts were accused of being witches or werewolves.

THE WEREWOLF OF DOLE

During the early sixteenth century, wolves began to invade France in great numbers. According to legend, these wolves were also shape-shifters who could be easily identified. In human form, the shifter would have a unibrow, meaning the presence of abundant hair between the eyebrows giving the appearance of one long eyebrow. Also, hair would grow on their palms, forcing them to shave. The use of a razor would result in them having rough palms. Thus anyone in sixteenth-century France who lived alone or in isolated areas in the countryside, whose appearance was disheveled, whose behavior was disagreeable, was easily suspected as a werewolf.

In a large number of accusations and arrests between 1520 and 1630, more than thirty thousand people in France alone were said to be werewolves and were brought to trial. Such was the fate of Gilles Garnier, a hermit and a peasant.

Garnier had a unibrow and lived outside the city of Dole. One night when villagers were rescuing a lost girl from the attack of a wolf, they claimed that they saw Garnier in the face of the beast. They accused him of becoming a wolf by rubbing a type of magic cream on his skin. A week after the rescue, Garnier was caught and taken into town. There he was beaten into a confession. He was found guilty of "crimes of lycanthropy and witchcraft" and burned at the stake on January 18, 1573.

Garnier's confession, however, was difficult to believe or prove. Interrogation processes then were cruel and included boiling the accused in oil and clawing them with hot pincers. Most people confessed quickly to avoid the horrible abuses.

In folklore, a full moon has the power to hypnotize man, luring him into frenzied behavior.

Moonstruck Lunatics

"Lunatic" comes from the French word *lune*, meaning the moon. From early times, human transformations into wolves have been linked to the full moon. Even as late as the early nineteenth century, the forces of the moon were often associated with temporary madness or wild behavior in humans. The moon is considered the ruling force of nature over werewolves and supernatural creatures of the night.

According to folklore, the light of the moon can induce seizures and insanity. This explains the terms "lunacy" and "**moonstruck**." Paracelsus, a sixteenth-century physician, said that the moon had "the power to tear reason out of a man's head by depriving him of humors and cerebral virtues."

Sir William Hale, a seventeenth-century chief justice in England, wrote: "The moon hath a great influence in all diseases of the brain … especially dementia; such person commonly in the full and change of the moon, especially about the equinoxes and summer solstice, are usually at the height of their distemper."

Eighteenth-century jurist Sir William Blackstone described a lunatic as someone who would "lose" or "enjoy" his reason, "depending on the changes of the moon."

As late as 1940, an English soldier charged with murdering his comrade pled "moon madness" as his defense. According to the soldier, this madness overtook him at each full moon. Perhaps he was an example of a modern-day werewolf?

Despite some studies having shown that emergency room visits and accidents are increased during the full moon period, modern science does not support the link between lunar phases and insanity.

Beware!
CARL LAEMMLE presents
WEREWOLF OF LONDON
with
Henry HULL - Warner OLAND
Valerie HOBSON Lester MATTHEWS
CLARK WILLIAMS · SPRING BYINGTON · LAWRENCE GRANT
Story by ROBERT HARRIS
produced by STANLEY BERGERMAN
A UNIVERSAL PICTURE

THE
SILVER SCREEN

"Even a man who is pure in heart and says his prayers by night may become a wolf when the wolfbane blooms and the autumn moon is bright."

JENNY WILLIAMS (PLAYED BY FAY HELM), *THE WOLF MAN* (1941)

EARLY TALES OF WEREWOLVES DATE BACK TO ancient folklore and Greek mythology. Stories of wolf-like creatures lunging from the darkness and savagely killing humans frightened people for centuries. Images of tormented souls doomed to become werewolves at the rising of a full moon were common and drove many to accuse and murder the innocent. Labeled as cursed and tortured by townspeople, werewolves have been a source of unending mystery throughout the ages. But it was Hollywood that plucked the beast and its myths from ancient times, bringing tales of humans turning into wolves into the twentieth century. Cinema has since kept legends of the werewolf alive.

Opposite: A poster from the 1935 film *Werewolf of London*

Cinematic Firsts

The first werewolf movie to enter the cinema was *The Werewolf*, opening in 1913. The black-and-white silent film was eighteen minutes in length and featured Clarence Burton as the werewolf. It was the only werewolf film that examined the folklore of Native American people who shifted into wolves through the use of magical powers. These lycans could also assume human form at will.

Drawing upon Navajo legends of witchcraft and shape-shifting, the film portrays a witch who turns her daughter into a werewolf so that she might attack the settlers invading their land. An actual wolf was used in the transformation sequences of this film, an effort involving simple camera dissolves, or cuts and fades to black. The film was destroyed in a fire at Universal Studios in 1924.

The silent French film *Le Loup Garou* (1923) was adapted from the Alfred Machard novel of the same name. This obscure black-and-white film tells the story of a murderer, Leon Bernier, who goes on the run with his young son. Not wanting to tell the boy the truth about his crimes, the father instead claims that a werewolf is chasing them. This movie too has been lost.

In 1925, George Chesebro directed and starred in the silent film *Wolfblood*. In the movie, Dick Bannister (played by Chesebro), a field boss for a Canadian logging crew, is hurt during a fight with employees of a rival logging company. Left for dead, Bannister needs a transfusion, but no one volunteers to help him. The doctor treating him is thereby forced to use the blood of a wolf. Bannister begins having nightmares in which he runs with a pack of phantom wolves, killing his rivals. When the news of his dreams gets out, the lumberjacks decide that Bannister is a werewolf. *Wolfblood* is often referenced as the first werewolf movie made, but as mentioned above, other films before it are on record.

The second adaptation of *Le Loup Garou*, known as the first "talking" werewolf film, *Gehetzte Menschen*, was released in 1932. In the original French novel, Vincent Olivier (Leon Bernier in the original adaptation) claims that he is being chased by *le loup garou*, meaning a werewolf. In this version of the story, however, he says he is chased by *der schwarze mann*, a German term meaning "bogey man." This, of course, removed the werewolf from the story. However, in the popular German children's game Who's Afraid of Der Schwarze Mann, the figure is more often referred to as the "big bad man" or "wolf man."

Henry Hull in full lycan makeup in *Werewolf of London*

The first full-length and mainstream Hollywood werewolf film was *Werewolf of London*. The movie starred Henry Hull as Dr. Wilfred Glendon and was produced by Universal Pictures in 1935. In the film, Dr. Glendon is a world-renowned botanist from London. He journeys to Tibet in search of the fictional Mariphasa plant, which only blooms in the moonlight. The sap from this plant has the power to counteract "werewolfery." The moment he finds the plant, Glendon is attacked and bitten by a wolf-like creature.

Later Glendon returns to London where he meets Dr. Yogami, who also suffered a wolf bite while in Tibet. Yogami, after confirming that Glendon too was in Tibet, asks for the plant as he does not want to suffer lycanthropy. Glendon refuses. He does not believe in werewolves; that is, until he himself transforms into a lycan and takes his first victim.

A Novel Idea

In 1933, Guy Endore published his work of historical fiction, *The Werewolf in Paris*. It is based on the life of Bertrand Caillet, a nineteenth-century shape-shifter who violated a number of graves throughout

Lon Chaney in full makeup in *The Wolf Man*

Paris before he was apprehended in 1840. To many, Caillet was a **ghoul**. But the way he mutilated corpses and committed acts of cannibalism later placed him in the category of werewolf. The novel was the inspiration for the 1961 film *The Curse of the Werewolf*, starring Oliver Reed.

Cinematic Dogma

The Wolf Man is a 1941 horror film (Universal). The title character has had a bit of influence on how Hollywood presents the legend of the werewolf. In fact, the movie created a number of lycan traditions that later became cinematic werewolf dogma—or something held as an established opinion. Some of these rules of lycanthropic behavior are:

- People become werewolves after being bitten or scratched by a werewolf.

- Upon the rising of the first full moon after the attack, the victim then experiences shape-shifting.

- A plant called wolfsbane keeps a werewolf at bay.

- An object made of silver is the only thing that can kill a werewolf.

With these rules, Universal rewrote centuries of werewolf lore and legend to satisfy growing audiences. The new dogma was never challenged—it was only enhanced for the dozens of werewolf characters and tales that followed.

The Good Wolf

Werewolves, both in folklore and the cinema, have been described as savage beasts roaming about searching for human flesh. But not all lycans were evil. Before religious leaders between the twelfth and the sixteenth centuries decided to condemn witches and werewolves, many were seen as good, sympathetic, or even **benevolent**. One such group is known as the Werewolves of Scotland. Their tale is part of the folklore of the Shetland Islands off the coast of Scotland.

Often called "Wulvers," the Werewolves of Scotland were known to be kindhearted. Generous to those in need, they left fish at the doors of widows and poor families. About the Wulvers, author Jessie Saxby wrote in *Shetland Traditional Lore*:

> The Wulver was a creature like a man with a wolf's head. He had short brown hair all over him. His home was a cave dug out of the side of a steep knowe, half-way up a hill. He didn't molest folk if folk didn't molest him. He was fond of fishing, and had a small rock in the deep water which is known to this day as the "Wulver's Stane." There he would sit fishing sillaks and piltaks for hour after hour. He was reported to have frequently left a few fish on the window-sill of some poor body.

A similarly passive werewolf is the *Faoladh* from Irish folklore. The Faoladh was said to have protected children and stood guard over wounded men.

6

GLOBAL LEGENDS

"If you look through the history books, you find that werewolves are far from a recent creation. But, frustratingly, many of the facts have been lost in the mists of time."

ANTHONY HEAD, ENGLISH ACTOR

OF ALL THE MYTHOLOGICAL CREATURES IN existence, the werewolf is the best known. Legends of the lycan are found in folklore worldwide. The exact point in history that marked the beginning of the tales is unknown. Many historians suggest that the original source is Greek mythology. Author Montague Summers, in his 1928 novel *The Werewolf*, implied that the Greeks adopted the idea of lycanthropy from an ancient Phoenician cult. Yet every culture has its unique beliefs, folklore, and myths about lycanthropy.

The Brothers Grimm

Jakob and Wilhelm Grimm, better known today as the Brothers Grimm, were German scholars who collected fairy tales. Together

Opposite: Tales of the werewolf are told worldwide.

they published *Grimm's Fairy Tales*, a famous collection of children's stories. In the volume of German legends the brothers collected in the early nineteenth century, the werewolf tale "I Would Have Eaten You Too" is presented. It soon became the most popular lycanthropic tale in Germany:

A soldier stated this story happened to his own grandfather. His grandfather went into the forest to cut wood with a friend and a third man. There was something strange about the third man, but the grandfather couldn't tell for sure what it was. After they had done their job and had become tired, the third man recommended they take a nap. Accordingly, the three men lay down on the ground and closed their eyes. The grandfather pretended to fall asleep, but actually kept his eyes slightly open. He was keen to find the reason behind the third man's strange behavior. The third man looked to see if the other two men were sleeping. When he was certain they were, he put on [or took off] a belt and became a wolf. But he didn't resemble a natural wolf. He looked rather different. He quickly ran off to a nearby field where he ambushed a pregnant female horse and devoured it completely. The man came back, took off [or put on] his belt, and lay down again in human form near the others. While returning to town, the third man complained about having a stomachache. As they entered the town gate, the grandfather whispered into the man's ear, "When one devours a whole horse … " But before he could finish his sentence, the third man interrupted, "Had you said this to me in the forest, you would not be able to say this now."

El Lobisón

When the words *el lobisón* are spoken in northern Argentina, the conversation is about a werewolf. The lobisón is usually the seventh son in a family. He would shift on the night of a full moon, especially if it fell on a Friday. This belief was especially strong in Argentina. The seventh daughter, however, is doomed to become a witch. The myth of the lobisón mainly prevails in Argentina, Brazil, Paraguay, and Uruguay.

A werewolf's dangerously sharp claws keep its victims from escaping.

When a lobisón shifts into a man-wolf creature, he wanders the hills and mountains and feeds mostly upon carrion, or dead and rotting flesh. Should a human cross the lobisón's path, the lobisón will attack. Any survivors will then become lobisónes. It is also said that if a lobisón spits on a person, then he or she will eventually become a lobisón, too.

By the early twentieth century, the legend of the seventh son (it had to be seven boys in a row, no girls in between) shifting into a lobisón had become widespread. This caused a great number of children to be abandoned or given away. Some parents would kill the seventh son. The belief in this myth was so strong that the Argentine president, Juan Domingo Perón (1895–1974), decreed that all seventh sons of a family must be baptized. This effort ended the days of people condemning their sons for fear of the lobisón.

The origin of the lobisón legend is found in Guarani mythology. The Guarani are the native people of Paraguay whose mythology stated there were seven monsters. Of the seven monsters, the last one, known as *Lusión*, was deformed but oddly did not resemble a wolf.

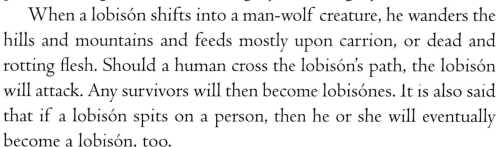

An Irish Tale of a Wolf

Ireland's tales of lycanthropy are said to be the most bizarre. Many blend the monsters into the legends of the saints. A popular werewolf story from twelfth-century Irish folklore involves a husband and wife and a priest:

A priest, accompanied by a boy, was traveling from Ulster to Meath. One night in the woods, a wolf approached the priest. As it came nearer, it began speaking. The priest became terrified and couldn't believe what he was seeing [or that the wolf was speaking]. The trembling priest asked the wolf what kind of creature was he that had the shape of a wolf but the words of a man. The wolf then told the priest that there was only one other creature like him and it was his wife … [H]is wife was very sick and dying. He was there to seek the priest's help in his wife's absolution—after all, they were just normal human beings under the wolf skin. Baffled and still terrified, the priest reluctantly followed the wolf … Sensing hesitation in the priest, and to assure him he wouldn't commit blasphemy by giving the dying wolf viaticum (holy bread), the male wolf peeled the skin of his ailing companion from the head down to the belly with his claw. Seeing a weak old woman underneath the hanging wolf-skin, the priest gave her the viaticum. Upon concluding the viaticum, the male wolf rolled the wolf-skin back over his wife's body. The old woman returned to her wolf form.

This story was documented as an instance rather than a mere myth, and was indexed in the **treatise** *Topographia Hibernica*, an account of the landscape and people of Ireland and their folklore.

HITLER'S FASCINATION

Adolf Hitler, leader of Nazi Germany from 1934 to 1945, held a deep fascination with werewolves. The very title "Führer" suggests the leader of a wolf pack. His first name, Adolph, means "noble wolf."

Numerous tales have spread about Hitler's so-called rages. He would fall to the floor and chew the carpet. According to psychobiographer Robert Waite, Hitler, at the beginning of his political career, had chosen "Herr Wolf" as his pseudonym, or fictitious name. His France-based headquarters were named *Woflsschluct*, meaning "wolf's gorge." In Ukraine, his administrative center was named *Werewolf*. Hitler then took his fascination with lycanthropy a step further, demanding that his sister change her name to Frau Wolf. He renamed the Volkswagen factory Wolfsburg and ordained himself Conductor Wolf. In fact, he was often heard whistling the tune "Who's Afraid of the Big Bad Wolf?"

Adolf Hitler with his German shepherd, Blondi

It was as werewolves that Hitler saw the *Hitlerjugend*, the youth in the educational program he dictated. Hitler demanded that the young boys become indifferent to pain, that they rid themselves of any weakness and tenderness. According to historians, when Hitler looked in their eyes he wanted to see "once more in the eyes of a pitiless youth the gleam of pride and independence of the beast of prey."

7

MODERN-DAY LYCANTHROPY

*"'Give the five signs that identify the werewolf.' Excellent question …
One: He's sitting on my chair. Two: He's wearing my clothes.
Three: His name's Remus Lupin … "*

REMUS LUPIN, *HARRY POTTER AND THE ORDER OF THE PHOENIX*

DECADES OF FOLKLORE, MYTH, AND literature have summoned various creatures and influenced how modern-day lycanthropy is presented. Although we tend to largely ignore the true existence of werewolves, or sometimes treat them as lesser terrors than vampires or zombies, their legends remain with us. They continue to lurk in the darkest corners of our mind and are ready to emerge at the slightest provocation as tales of lycanthropy follow us through the twenty-first century.

MODERN CREATURES IN LITERATURE AND FILM

In 2004, author Stephenie Meyer launched her vampire series, the Twilight Saga. *Twilight*, the first in the book collection, was released

Opposite: In the Twilight series, shape-shifter Jacob Black (played by Taylor Lautner) transforms into a wolf.

Remus Lupin (*far right*) was a half-blood wizard afflicted with lycanthropy during his childhood.

as a motion picture in 2008. While the series is mostly a romance between Bella Swan, a mortal, and Edward Cullen, a vampire, it does introduce a werewolf, Jacob Black, and his clan.

When Meyer imagined the appearance of the werewolves in her series, she wanted to forego the man-wolf beasts depicted in most Hollywood films. She created instead horse-sized wolves with only their human eyes to betray them. When Bella first encounters the werewolves in the meadow, she sees the eyes of Jacob Black in one of the wolves. The wolves Meyer created also differ in the form of shifting.

The *Twilight* werewolves, in order to shift, have to be a direct descendent of Taha Aki, the spirit chief and the first shape-shifter of the Quileute tribe (as is Jacob), or indirectly (as with another werewolf character named Embry). It is believed that the wolf gene is passed on between father and son, and can be latent, or dormant, with one generation. Meyer's werewolves can also transform at any time. They tend to shift more during times when they express extreme emotion—anger being the strongest trigger.

The popularity and creative changes in the depictions of werewolves in both literature and film opened the door for J. K. Rowling's Harry Potter series to introduce Remus J. Lupin—the full-fledged werewolf who appeared in *The Prisoner of Azkaban*.

Remus takes the form of an ill and quiet yet powerful wizard. He is Harry's Defense Against the Dark Arts teacher. Lupin became cursed as a werewolf for life when his father refused to be bullied by the savage werewolf Fenrir Greyback. In an act of revenge, Greyback attacked Remus as a small child, and purposely spared Remus's life so that his family would suffer. In Rowling's universe werewolves are hated, even ostracized from the modern witch society. Thus Remus's family goes through great lengths to keep his lycanthropy a secret.

Wolves must keep a low-key existence in some other societies as well. The werewolves in the HBO series *True Blood*, for example, do not have the same freedom to move about as the vampires. They must remain hidden because of their full-moon transformation.

It was season three of *True Blood* when a werewolf, Alcide Herveaux, was introduced into the show's cast of supernatural characters. In true werewolf fashion, Herveaux shifts into a live wolf: a giant North American timber wolf with yellow eyes. The series also brought in witches, a family of were-panthers, and revealed that the lead character, Sookie Stackhouse, comes from fairy heritage.

The Evolution of Young Wolves

To continue the burgeoning teen-horror movie genre, Hollywood began to produce young lycan films. The first: *I Was a Teenage Werewolf* (1959). The starring wolf, played by Michael Landon, was neither bitten nor scratched by a lycan. He shifted into a werewolf in the classic tradition: at the hands of an evil sorcerer—an unscrupulous psychiatrist, in this case. The success of this film spurred the making of *I Was a Teenage Frankenstein* (1957), *Blood of Dracula* (1957), and *How to Make a Monster* (1958). But television took a turn in 1964 when CBS created a clean-cut and humorous version of a boy werewolf in their series *The Munsters*: Edward "Eddie" Wolfgang Munster, played by Butch Patrick.

Humanizing Monsters

The Munsters (aired 1964–1966) depicted a family of paranormal creatures that included a father, Herman, who looked like Frankenstein's monster (Fred Gwynne); a vampire mother, Lily (Yvonne De Carlo); and a Count Dracula–style grandfather, Grandpa (Al Lewis). Although Eddie was a werewolf, in some episodes he would show signs of vampire behavior. He had fangs that were actually his own teeth, which Patrick said "stuck out over my lips so they looked natural." The family lived at 1313 Mockingbird Lane in the city of Mockingbird Heights, a fictional California suburb.

In the 1985 film *Teen Wolf*, Michael J. Fox took on the role of a high school student who inherited lycanthropy from his father. Although the film did not have great success, a television series adapted from the film, *Teen Wolf*, debuted in 2011.

Werewolves in *Buffy the Vampire Slayer* (aired 1997–2003) were usually afflicted with lycanthropy through a bite. Shifters in this series transformed into wolf-like creatures at sunset on the three nights when the moon was nearest full. They would then revert to human form at dawn. Although they portrayed specific animal characteristics, their appearances as wolves closely resembled their appearances as humans.

Today werewolves continue to be popular supernatural characters in TV shows. For example, *The Vampire Diaries* (2009–present) and its spin-off show, *The Originals* (2013–present), feature different werewolf families who must choose between joining good or evil. As with every new version of werewolves in modern society, more legends and abilities are added to their ever-expanding mythology.

A Search for the Truth

Over the years, researchers have developed theories to explain the episodes of lycanthropy in eighteenth- and nineteenth-century Europe. One such explanation is ergot, a disease of rye and other cereal grains caused by a fungus.

Ergot can affect an entire town, causing hallucinations, mass hysteria, and paranoia, as well as convulsions and sometimes death. Some researchers presented the argument that ergot poisoning can convince its victim that he or she is a wolf. It can also cause an entire town to believe that they have seen a werewolf. This theory, however, is controversial and not well accepted.

Some modern researchers argue that conditions such as rabies, hypertrichosis (excessive hair growth over the entire body), and an enzyme disorder with symptoms including hallucinations and paranoia explain werewolf beliefs and behaviors. There is also a rare mental disorder called clinical lycanthropy. The person suffering this disorder has a delusional belief that he or she is transforming into another animal. Others believe werewolf legends came about as a part of **shamanism** and totem animals in primitive and nature-based cultures. With so many different theories and assumptions as to the origin of the werewolf, exactly where the legend started may never be known.

Among many in today's society, a silent fear of the beast still lingers. Lycans are not always a great distance from the streets of a busy city or the remote and shadowy forest. And no one knows what lurks in the shade beneath low-hanging tree branches. Werewolves may be far closer to us than we would prefer.

Glossary

amuck In an undisciplined, uncontrolled, or faulty manner.

benevolent Organized for the purpose of doing good.

bestiary A collection of descriptions or representations of real or imaginary animals.

canid Any of a family of carnivorous animals that includes wolves, jackals, foxes, coyotes, and the domestic dog.

cannibalism The ritualistic eating of human flesh by a human being.

carnivorous Subsisting or feeding on animal tissues.

counterfeiting To imitate or feign, especially with intent to deceive.

cunning Characterized by wiliness and trickery; clever or sly.

ecosystem A community of living organisms (plants, animals, and microbes) in conjunction with the nonliving components of their environment (air, water, and mineral soil), interacting as a system.

fossil record The history of life as documented by fossils, meaning the remains or imprints of the organisms from earlier geological periods preserved in sedimentary rock.

ghoul A phantom, especially one who robs graves and feeds on dead bodies.

heinous Hateful or shockingly evil.

heresy An opinion or doctrine contrary to church dogma.

lycan A second breed of werewolves created in the eleventh century.

lycanthropy The delusion that one has become a wolf.

moonstruck Affected by, or changed as if by, the moon.

moor An expanse of open rolling infertile land; a boggy area.

predatory Living by killing and eating other animals.

sever To remove by cutting.

shamanism An ancient healing tradition and way of life; a shaman is a medicine man or woman.

shape-shifter One with the ability to change form or identity at will; a mythical figure that can assume different forms.

totemism The belief in kinship with or a mystical relationship between a group or an individual and a totem.

treatise A written work dealing formally and systematically with a subject.

unguent A soft, greasy substance used as an ointment or for lubrication.

Vikings Members of the Scandinavian seafaring warriors who raided and colonized wide areas of Europe from the ninth to the eleventh century. Also called Norsemen or Northmen.

To Learn More About Werewolves

Books

Amin, Ibrahim. *The Monster Hunter Handbook: The Ultimate Guide to Saving Mankind from Vampires, Zombies, Hellhounds, and Other Mythical Beasts.* London: Bloomsbury, 2007.

Curran, Robert. *The Werewolf Handbook: An Essential Guide to Werewolves and, More Importantly, How to Avoid Them.* Hauppauge, NY: Barron's Educational Series, 2010.

Wolff, Becky. *Werewolves!* Kids Look and Learn! Seattle, WA: Amazon Digital Services, 2013.

Website

Kids Net

encyclopedia.kids.net.au/page/we/Werewolf

Learn more about the history of werewolves and their scientific background, and discover werewolves in modern fiction.

Video

In Search of History: Legends of the Werewolves

www.youtube.com/watch?v=HCHZjU7Hi0w

Watch this full-length documentary about the one of the most ancient and enduring legends: the werewolf. From the History Channel.

BIBLIOGRAPHY

Baring-Gould, Sabine. *The Book of Were-Wolves*. San Bernardino, CA: Forgotten Books, 2008.

Charles VII. *Chronique*. Paris: Chez P. Jannet, Librarie, 1858.

Curran, Bob. *Encyclopedia of the Undead: A Field Guide to Creatures that Cannot Rest in Peace*. Franklin Lakes, NJ: New Page Books, 2006.

Guiley, Rosemary. *The Encyclopedia of Vampires, Werewolves, and Other Monsters*. New York: Facts on File, 2005.

Konstantinos. *Werewolves: The Occult Truth*. Woodbury, MN: Llewellyn Publications, 2010.

Krull, Manning Leonard. "The Wolves of Paris." *Cool Stuff in Paris*. www.coolstuffin paris.com/wolves_of_paris.php.

Otten, Charlotte F. *The Literary Werewolf: An Anthology*. Syracuse, NY: Syracuse University Press, 2002.

Perrault, Charles. "Little Red Riding Hood." Accessed February 1, 2015. *University of Pittsburgh*. www.pitt.edu/~dash/perrault02.html.

Saxby, Jessie M.E. *Shetland Traditional Lore*. Edinburgh, Scotland: Grant & Murray, 1932.

Schwalb, Suzanne, and Margaret Rubiano. *Vampires, Werewolves, Zombies: Compendium Monstrum*. White Plains, NY: Peter Pauper Press, 2010.

Steiger, Brad. *The Werewolf Book: The Encyclopedia of Shape-Shifting Beings*. Canton, MI: Visible Ink Press, 2012.

Stewart, Caroline Taylor. *The Origin of the Werewolf Superstition*. Columbia, MO: University of Missouri, 1909.

Summers, Montague. *The Werewolf in Lore and Legend*. Mineola, NY: Dover Publications, 1933.

Index

Page numbers in **boldface** are illustrations. Entries in **boldface** are glossary terms.

ABOUT THE AUTHOR

Cynthia A. Roby is the author of several fictional short stories as well as nonfiction books for young readers. She has been a fan of werewolf movies since she discovered *The Wolf Man* (1941), starring Lon Chaney Jr., while in the second grade. Roby currently lives in Bronx, New York, with her two cats, Peter Tosh and Toni Morrison.

DATE DUE

3-25